THE RISE AND RISE OF CHINA

NICOLE LYONS

WHERE DOES CHINA GO FROM HERE?

KS3 GEOGRAPHY TEACHERS' TOOLKIT

EDITED BY ALAN KINDER AND JOHN WIDDOWSON

ISBN 978 1 84377 212 5
First published 2008
Impression number 10 9 8 7 6 5 4 3 2 1
Year 2011 2010 2009

Published by the Geographical Association, 160 Solly Street, Sheffield S1 4BF.
Website: www.geography.org.uk
E-mail: info@geography.org.uk
The Geographical Association is a registered charity: no 313129

The GA would be happy to hear from other potential authors who have ideas for geography books. You may contact the Publications Officer via the GA at the address above.

Edited by Andrew Shackleton
Designed by Bryan Ledgard
Printed and bound in China through Colorcraft Ltd, Hong Kong

CONTENTS

EDITORS' PREFACE

The *KS3 Geography Teacher's Toolkit* is designed to help teach the new key stage 3 curriculum from 2008. The series draws on the Key Concepts, Key Processes and Curriculum Opportunities in the new Programme of Study and applies these to selected parts of the Range and Content. For teachers, it provides timely guidance on meeting the challenge of creating and teaching the curriculum. Each title in the series illustrates ways of exploring a place, theme or issue of interest to young people and of geographical significance in the twenty-first century. The selection of content is carefully explained, ideas are clearly linked to the new Programme of Study and advice is provided on the use of teaching strategies to engage and challenge all learners in the classroom.

The *Toolkit* can be used in a number of ways. For busy teachers of geography, under pressure from curriculum change throughout the secondary phase, each title in this series provides a complete unit of work: a bank of ready-made lesson plans and accompanying resources. These materials can be used *directly* in the classroom, with minimal preparation. The printed resources in each book may be copied directly, but complete resources for every lesson are contained on the easy-to-navigate CD.

Toolkit materials can also be extended. Each title provides links to websites of interest and to further resources and reading, encouraging teachers and students to 'dig deeper' into their chosen places, themes and issues. Activities within each unit can be extended into full-scale enquiries, to stretch even the highest attainers.

The *Toolkit* has also been designed to be adapted. Teaching strategies are explained throughout each book, allowing teachers to understand the 'how to' of each lesson activity. It is hoped that teachers using these materials will be encouraged to select ideas, change them to meet the needs of their own learners, and begin to use relevant teaching strategies elsewhere in their curriculum. Each title is therefore a rich source of teacher-to-teacher advice, a 'professional development' resource that can be used to inform the teaching of places, themes and issues of your own choosing.

Lastly, the series provides a template for writing new curriculum materials. Unit summaries, concept maps linked to new Key Concepts, assessment frameworks, glossaries, lesson plans and other materials are included as exemplars of rigorous curriculum planning.

By using, extending, selecting and adapting appropriate 'tools' from the *Toolkit*, teachers will gain confidence in developing their own materials and creating a high-quality curriculum suited to the needs and interests of their learners. We hope that the series will help teachers fully exploit the rich potential of the new KS3 Programme of Study.

Alan Kinder and John Widdowson, 2008.

1. ABOUT THE RISE AND RISE OF CHINA

Why teach about China?

All change!

Geography is a subject which, uniquely, adapts and changes in response to the way the world is changing. At its radical best, geography can successfully engage students by reflecting the world that they are growing up in. Nowhere in the world is changing faster than China. Its status and characteristics change with each generation. As a young teacher, I am amazed by the fact that in the few years that have passed since I was a student, my knowledge of China has become out of date. You may wonder whether it is worth teaching students about a country that is changing so fast. But the rate of change is, in itself, a reason why it is important for students to learn about China. Teaching students about the process of change, using China as a case study, will help students to understand the dynamic nature of geography.

China is emerging as a modern superpower

Learning about China offers students the opportunity to study the geography of a single country. However, China is not just any country. It is home to a quarter of the world's population and is likely to overtake the USA as the world's largest economy some time in the next 40 years. Economic growth and political relationships are complex, but important for students to consider, if they are to understand the changes which are occurring in the world. China exemplifies how economics and politics interact (Figure 1), nationally and internationally. Studying China illustrates for students both the changing distribution of wealth within a country and changes at the global level.

China is closer to the UK than we think

Studying other places often helps students to put their own place into perspective. In this case, the changes happening in China will help students to reflect on changes in the UK. We want students to view China as a country where similar geographical processes happen to here, rather than as a separate entity. China has many links with the UK, yet at the same time its culture is in stark contrast to ours. China presents an excellent opportunity for students to make connections with a country which in many ways is so different from the place where we live, yet in other ways is closer than we think.

Figure 1: Economics and politics exemplified on China's currency. Photo: Kevin Connors/Morguefile.

How to teach about China

Use images

Most students will never have had the opportunity to visit China. It is vital to use images – both moving and still – to give a sense of place and to bring the data about China to life. Images can be viewed subjectively. This allows students to develop their own sense of place, and to build on their geographical imaginations of places.

Images are an invaluable tool for prompting discussion in the classroom. Students may not have first-hand experience of China but they will be able to describe 'what is happening' in a photograph and express their own opinions about images. Images can be used to paint a picture of China, and to show the diversity within the country.

Promote discussion

With so many changes occurring and issues arising in China, there is no shortage of opportunities to encourage students to develop their discussion skills as a way of building confidence and personal knowledge. Many students find it difficult to develop an 'opinion' or 'argument' about an issue. However, it is still important to address difficult and, sometimes, controversial issues, such as climate change or immigration.

Discussion needs to be structured so students become comfortable expressing their views. For example, students can sort statements according to the extent to which they agree or disagree with them, and discuss with other students why their arrangement is different. In this way they begin to build up enough confidence to present their own argument or produce a piece of extended writing.

Another skill which students often lack is the ability to present two opposing views. They tend to look for the 'right answers'. By working in pairs, representing different opinions, students can discuss issues in an informal setting. They will start to build up their own, independent knowledge and views of an issue.

It is equally important that we create an atmosphere where students feel that they can ask questions. I often encourage this by asking all students to ask one question about an image, a person, or a piece of text.

Photo © Kevin Connors/Morguefile

Encourage critical thinking

We need to encourage students to view information critically and we should do this from an early stage. Critical thinking techniques are often applied at key stages 4 and 5, but not so commonly at key stage 3. In this unit, political opinions, news articles and statistical data are used as sources of information about China. It is important that students consider the reliability of these sources, and that we encourage them to think independently about what they are learning. In this way we demonstrate to students that information is subjective and dynamic. Without thinking critically, students' knowledge of China would be two-dimensional. Above all, this unit aims to encourage students to learn to view information critically, realise that there are alternative interpretations and express their own views.

Summary

This is primarily a unit about place. Students study China as a place where change is happening. They consider the similarities and differences between the UK and China, and how and why these may change in the future. Through the unit students also investigate the key concepts of interdependence and sustainability. Students begin to evaluate information critically.

Prior learning

In key stage 2, students have studied 'places' and will already be familiar with some aspects of what 'makes a place', e.g. population, landscape, culture. Students have developed numeracy skills to enable them to interpret data, and this unit develops these skills.

Future learning

By GCSE, students become increasingly familiar with the ways in which geographical processes interact to bring about change. With growing confidence, they will evaluate information critically and distinguish fact and opinion to develop their own ideas – key skills at GCSE level.

Key learning outcomes

Most students will be able to:

- learn about China's characteristics, and how these may change in the future
- understand how China is related to their lives, and to other places and people in the world
- critically evaluate information about China
- use facts and opinions to help them to develop their own ideas.

Some students will not have made so much progress but will be able to:

- learn key information about China
- understand how China is linked with their lives.

Some students will have progressed further and will be able to:

- understand the ways in which people and the environment interact in China
- make suggestions about the future of China and the impact this might have on their own lives.

Photo © Kevin Rosseel/Morguefile

The geography behind China

The graphs in Figure 2 show how quickly the position of China and other emerging nations will change in the future.

BRIC is a term that refers to Brazil, Russia, India and China – four countries currently experiencing fast growth and development.

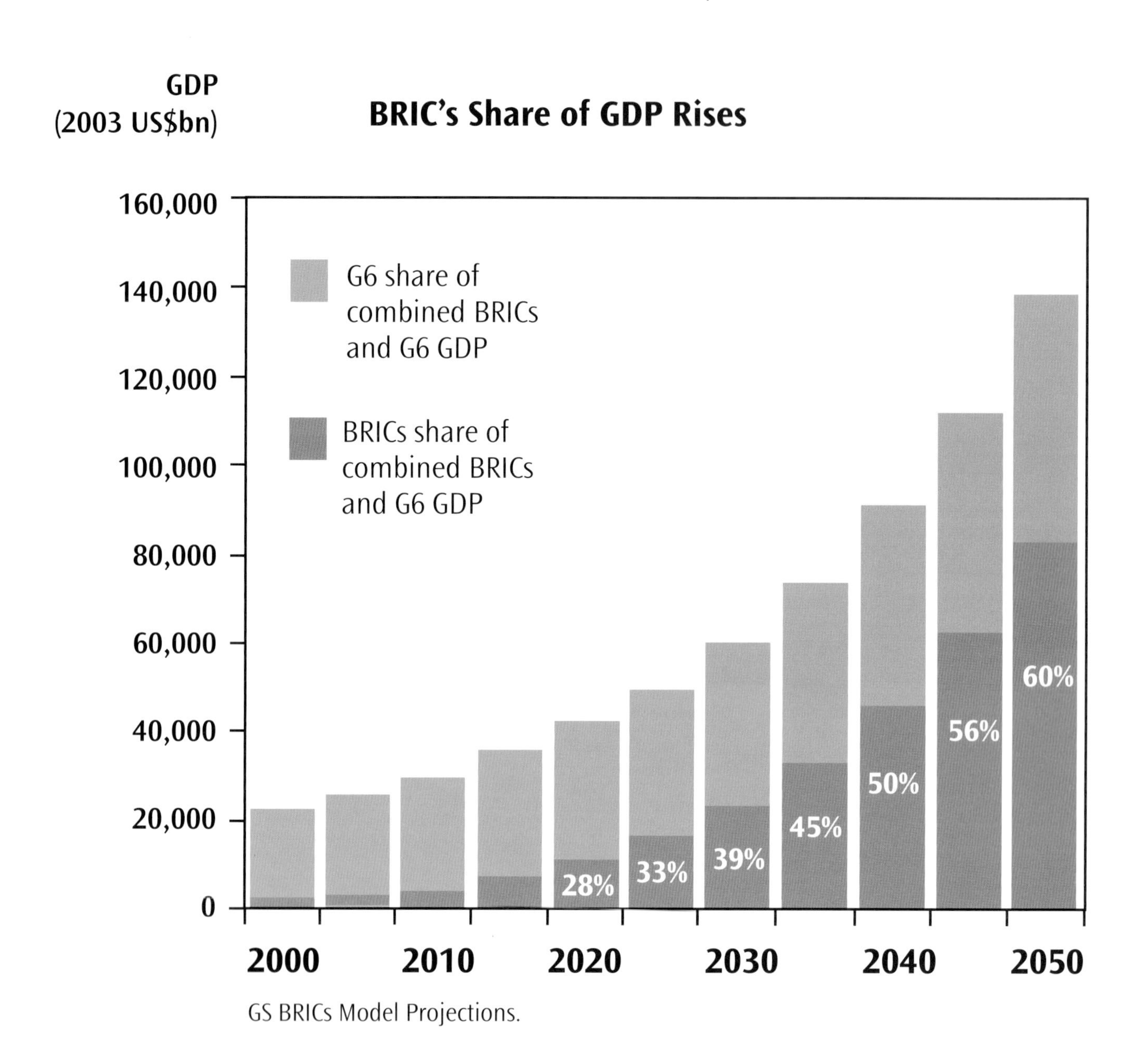

Figure 2: China's expected position in the future. Source: Goldman Sachs, 2003.

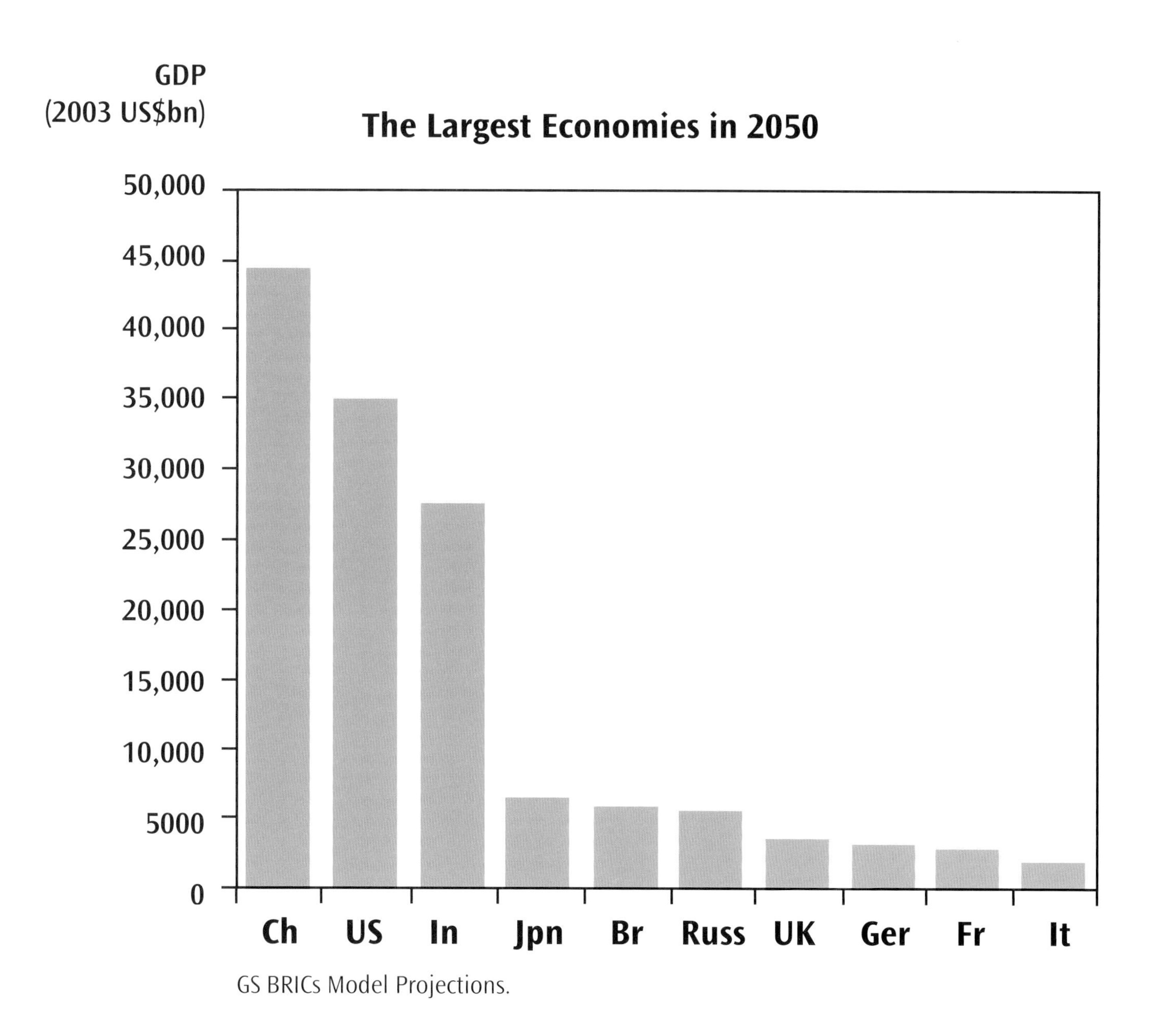

GS BRICs Model Projections.

The Rise and Rise of China: Concept map

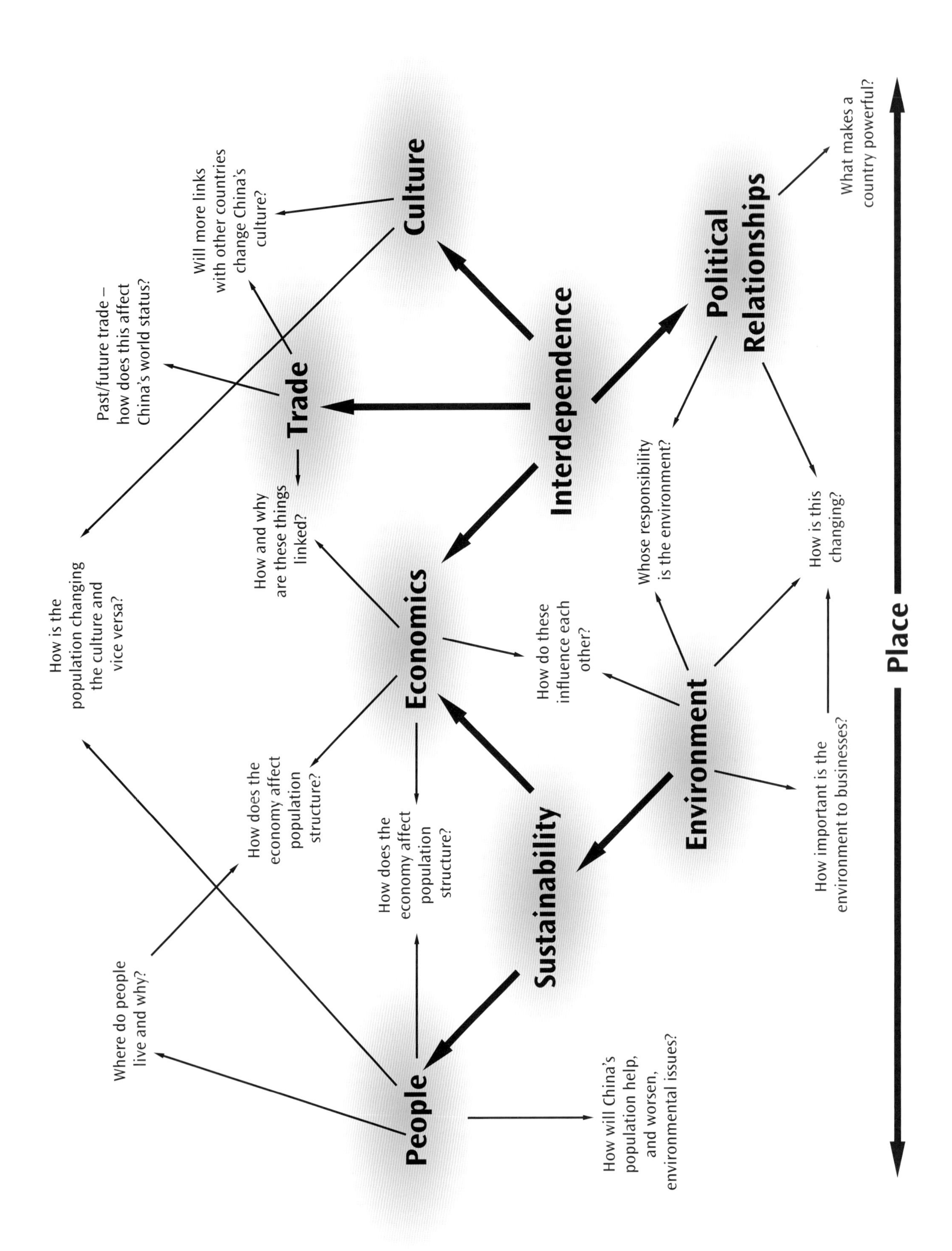

Links to the revised Programme of Study

Key concepts

Place

This unit:

- studies China at a variety of scales
- helps students to understand the depth and diversity of the country.

Interdependence

This unit:

- looks at the ways in which China is linked to the rest of the world through tourism, culture and trade.

Environmental interaction and sustainable development

This unit:

- explores the interaction between human and physical aspects of China's geography
- explores how China can develop sustainably.

Key processes

Enquiry

This unit:

- focuses students on the central enquiry question 'Where does China go from here?'.

Graphicacy

This unit:

- employs maps, images and statistical data to develop students' knowledge and understanding of China.

Communication

This unit:

- encourages students to express their opinions through discussion and in writing.

Range and content

This unit:

- examines China at the local, regional and national scales
- investigates China in the context of its growing importance as a world superpower
- focuses on the process of development and change in China
- considers the interaction between people and environment in China, and its significance for the rest of the world.

2: THE RISE AND RISE OF CHINA
Medium-term plan

Lesson	Key questions	Learning objectives	Teaching and learning	Resources	Assessment opportunities
1	What do we know about China? What are the important characteristics of a country?	To know some of the main characteristics of China To understand how countries differ To appreciate that people may view the same place differently	Focus on what students already know about China. They use the information to draw a map Students play the Country Association game Students sort information about China into categories. They use information to make an annotated map of China Class discussion about how we use maps	Activity Sheet 1 Activity Sheet 2 Activity Sheet 3 Atlases	Students construct a map of China with a key
2	Where does our information about China come from? Which types of information are the most reliable? Why should we try to view information critically?	To be able to use the internet for research purposes To understand that not all information is equally reliable To find new and up-to-date information about China	Focus on internet research on China to find more information and to consider its reliability Students sort sources of information according to their reliability Students choose four independent enquiry questions, then visit a Chinese information website to find the answers. They write a review of the website Students feed back what they have learned about China and how reliable they think the information is	Activity Sheet 4 Activity Sheet 5 Information Sheet 1 Glue ICT facilities for students to carry out internet research	Students create enquiry questions and answer them through the lesson
3	Where do people live in China? Why do people choose to live in certain places?	To be able to show how population is distributed on a map in China To understand why population in China is distributed this way	Focus on making a 3D population distribution map of China and trying to explain the distribution Demonstrate to students the concept of population distribution using space in the classroom Students use Lego bricks to make a 3D population distribution map. They analyse the distribution on the map. They use a physical map to try to explain the distribution Students match cities with populations to compare China and the UK	Activity Sheet 6 (enlarged to A3 size) Information Sheet 2 Activity Sheet 7 Information Sheet 3 Information Sheet 4 Information Sheet 5 Lego bricks (sugar	Students make a 3D population distribution map, then analyse it

Lesson	Key questions	Learning objectives	Teaching and learning	Resources	Assessment opportunities
3 cont.				cubes, marshmallows or coins may make suitable alternatives) Colouring pencils Atlases Digital camera	
4	How is China linked with the rest of the world?	To know how China is linked with other countries in the world To understand that closer relationships with other countries will aid China's development	Focus on the different ways in which China is linked with the rest of the world and students' personal links Students compare the Great Wall of China, a symbol of China's former isolation, with an extract about China's modern links Students read about China's links with the rest of world. They use these to construct a world map of China's links Students think about their own personal links with China and each share one of these	Information Sheet 6 Information Sheet 7 Information Sheet 8 Activity Sheet 8 Atlases	Students explain how they are linked to China
5	How does China compare with other countries? What are the characteristics of MEDCs and LEDCs?	To know the characteristics of MEDCs and LEDCs To be able to compare China's level of development with that of other countries	Focus on indicators of development and where China falls on the spectrum from LEDC to MEDC Students identify the main indicators of development Students play 'Top Trumps' for 20 countries, making observations about development as they do so. The class discuss what they have observed during the game. Students answer structured questions about China's level of development Students look at Worldmapper maps showing China's changing wealth 1990-2015	Activity Sheet 9 Activity Sheet 10 Activity Sheet 11 Information Sheet 9 Information Sheet 10	Students contribute to class discussion Students write a paragraph about development and how China compares with other countries

Lesson	Key questions	Learning objectives	Teaching and learning	Resources	Assessment opportunities
6	How is China developing?	To be able to recognise evidence of China's development To understand how China's economy is likely to change in the future	Focus on photographic evidence of China's development to create a photostory Students discuss the meaning of a cartoon that shows China overtaking other countries Students look at a series of photos of China's development then match photos and statements and arrange them into a photostory Students study a graph showing the BRIC economies overtaking the G6 countries and discuss a set of questions	Figure 3 from CD Activity Sheet 12 Activity Sheet 13 Information Sheet 11 Figures 4-10 from CD	Students present a photostory to illustrate how China is developing
7	How sustainable is China's development? What is sustainability?	To understand the concept of sustainability To know the advantages and disadvantages of the Three Gorges Dam project To be able to form a balanced opinion about an issue	Focus on the concept of sustainability and how this is applicable to the Three Gorges Dam project Students read and compare definitions of sustainability to construct their own definition Students read an article about the Three Gorges Dam project. They highlight advantages and disadvantages and transfer these to opinion scales. They write a balanced opinion about how successful the project has been The class listen to each other's opinions	Activity Sheet 14 Activity Sheet 15 Red and green pens/pencils Activity Sheet 16 Activity Sheet 17 Information Sheet 12	Students write their balanced opinion of the Three Gorges Dam project
8	Is there a more sustainable option for China?	To understand how the Dongtan Eco-City project is designed to be sustainable To be able to critically evaluate the Dongtan Eco-City project	Focus on evaluating the sustainability of the Dongtan Eco-City project Students try to solve the mystery: How will rice husks help China to become more sustainable? Introduce students to the Dongtan Eco-City project. They write a letter about moving to Dongtan, in which they evaluate the project Students look at a cartoon of London. They discuss how UK cities could be more sustainable	Information Sheet 13 Activity Sheet 18 London cartoon at http://hello.eboy.com/eboy/?p=197	Students write a letter to describe the city of Dongtan and evaluate the project
9	Should China try to reduce its energy consumption?	To know the world's biggest economies, populations and consumers of energy	Focus on comparison of countries' wealth, population and energy consumption and opinions about levels of energy consumption Students try to guess the top ten largest economies, populations and energy	Information Sheet 14 Space (in classroom or outside) to make an opinion line	Students write a speech on how the UK should respond to China's energy consumption levels

Lesson	Key questions	Learning objectives	Teaching and learning	Resources	Assessment opportunities
9 cont.	How are economy, population and energy consumption linked?	To understand how economy, population and energy consumption are linked To be able to express opinions about levels of energy consumption	consumers. They compare countries using Worldmapper maps Students choose positions on an opinion line in response to statements about energy consumption. They write a short Prime Minister's speech about how the UK is going to respond to China's greenhouse gas emissions Students share their ideas and compare them to the Kyoto Protocol	Information Sheet 15 Information Sheet 16	
10	How and why is China likely to change in the future? What will geography teachers say about China in 20 years' time?	To understand how China's characteristics might change To understand how China's relationship with other countries may change in the future	Focus on paired images of China that show how it is changing, and may change in the future Students look at paired images that illustrate how China is changing. They refer back to the list of China's characteristics that they wrote in lesson 1. They use these to create a mind map showing how each characteristic is changing Students present a lesson about China in the future, using their mind map	Copy of list of country characteristics created during the starter activity in lesson 1 A3 paper for mind map Information Sheet 17 Information Sheet 18	Students contribute to class discussion on how China may change Students create a mind map to show how China's characteristics might change

LESSON 1: What do we know about China?

Key questions
- What do we know about China?
- What are the important characteristics of a country?

Key words
- physical
- human
- environmental

Resources
- Activity Sheet 1
- Activity Sheet 2
- Activity Sheet 3
- Atlases

Learning objectives
- To know some of the main characteristics of China
- To understand how countries differ
- To appreciate that people may view the same place differently

Assessment opportunities
- Students construct a map of China, with a key

Starter
Tell students to work with a partner. Hand out a set of cards from Activity Sheet 1 to each pair. Students play the Country Association Game. One student in the pair picks up a card and names the country. The other student then says the first thing that comes into his or her head (e.g. 'USA?' or 'Disney') and records it. Students take turns, in their pairs, to name a country and say what it makes them think of, until they have gone through the set of cards.

Students feed back their responses to the whole class. As they respond, list the characteristics they mention on the board. Ask students to suggest categories into which they could place the characteristics (e.g. food, landmarks, tourism, wealth, people, culture, media). Keep this list on display throughout the lesson and keep a record of it to refer to during the last lesson of this unit.

It may be necessary to discuss what comments are appropriate within this game. The activity does not ask for students' opinions of a country, but what they most commonly associate with that country.

Main teaching and learning phase
Introduce China to students. Ask them what they already know about China, e.g. 'How big is it?', 'How many people live there?', 'What language do they speak?'. Hand out sets of cards from Activity Sheet 2. Ask students to work in groups of two or three to sort the cards into the same categories that they created during the starter. It may be necessary for students to create new categories for some information.

When students have sorted all the cards, and are happy with their decisions, they make an annotated map of China on Activity Sheet 3. They use the information on the cards and in the atlases to do this. For example, they can draw the main physical and human features of China onto the map (rivers, cities etc.). Students may find more creative ways to add other information to the map. Some of the information will be difficult to map, and some will be impossible!

In this section of the lesson you may need to clear up some 'myths' about China – students may have outdated or incorrect knowledge. Use some of the websites recommended at the end of this title to check up on any issues that you are unsure about.

Plenary/review
Lead a whole-class discussion based on the mapping task. Use the questions below to guide the discussion.

- Why do we use maps?
- What are we able to map?
- What things are easy to map?
- What things are difficult to map?
- Is there anything that is impossible to map?

Throughout the discussion encourage students to reflect upon their own maps, and how they could use maps in the future.

KS3 GEOGRAPHY TEACHERS' TOOLKIT: THE RISE AND RISE OF CHINA

LESSON 1: Activity Sheet 2

China information

There are three main rivers in China – the Yangtze, Huang He and Pearl Rivers	Beijing is the capital of China
A great flat plain lies to the north-west of China	One of the most famous landmarks in is the Great Wall of China, the longest man-made structure in the world, stretching nearly 7000km long
China is one of the world's oldest civilisations, thought to date back to 6000 years ago	Most of China's population speak Mandarin, although there are also many regional languages spoken throughout the country
Rice is the main staple food in China	China is a communist country
China used to be an LEDC, but the country is quickly developing as a result of foreign investment in the country	The east coast of China borders the Pacific Ocean
The currency used in China is Yuan	The Gobi Desert is situated in the northern part of China
Most of China's population lives in the south-east of the country	Main cities in China include Beijing, Shanghai and **[??? Nicole please complete]**
hina has a population of 1.3 billion (2007) – the argest population of any country in the world	China is a large country containing many different climates. The north is cold and dry, and the south is warmer and wetter
he Himalayan Mountains are found in the outh- west of China and run along China's border with Nepal and India	Restaurants in the UK serve food which is Chinese in origin but adapted to the tastes of customers. Sweet and Sour Chicken is an example of a westernised Chinese food

Photos © Bryan Ledgard.

LESSON 2: Where does our information about China come from?

Key questions

- Where does our information about China come from?
- Which types of information are the most reliable?
- Why should we try to view information critically?

Key words

- reliability
- relevance
- source

Resources

- Activity Sheet 4
- Activity Sheet 5
- Information Sheet 1
- Glue
- ICT facilities for students to carry out internet research

Learning objectives

- To be able to use the internet for research purposes
- To understand that not all information is equally reliable
- To find new and up-to-date information about China

Assessment opportunities

- Students create enquiry questions and then answer them through the lesson

Starter

Hand out a set of cards from Activity Sheet 4 to each student. They sort the 'sources of information' in order of reliability. They place them on their desk from the most reliable on the left to the least reliable on the right. Discuss with the class why students chose to put the cards in that order.

> You could model for students how the use of connectives (because, therefore, however, so etc.) can help them to write an explanation.

Students stick the cards down in order of reliability. They add notes to explain their choices.

Main teaching and learning phase

Hand out Information Sheet 1. Ask students to choose a website where they can find information about China.

> Alternatively, you could ask them to find a website by using an internet search engine. It is important to give students strict time limits for internet work, to prevent them from becoming distracted.

Students complete the website review on Activity Sheet 5 for the site that they choose. First, and most important, students think of four enquiry questions and write these down. Some students may find it difficult to think of sophisticated questions. If so, encourage them to think of simple questions about China that the website may be able to answer. Before choosing their questions, students need to know what kind of website they are visiting (e.g. tourist board, national statistics etc.). Students then try to find the answers to their questions on the website, and complete the rest of the activity sheet.

> If there are not enough computers for students to use in the classroom, then print a selection of different web pages that you have found yourself. Alternatively, provide other sources of information such as textbooks, newspaper articles or atlases. You would need to change, or omit, some questions on the worksheet.

Plenary/review

Students feed back their experience of doing the research to the whole class. They rate how useful they found their website. Ask each student to contribute one thing that they have learned about China from the lesson, and to say how reliable they think the information is.

> The information gathered through the lesson could be displayed on a board/door/wall in the classroom on sticky notes or similar, and could be added to throughout the unit.

Chinese information websites

China

An online encyclopaedic account of China and its history. The site contains many useful links to articles and websites for further research. Please be aware that wikipedia entries are contributed by the public, and are not closely regulated
http://en.wikipedia.org/wiki/China

China National Tourist Office

China's official tourist site. Contains information about new developments in China's tourist industry, as well as introductory information on the country
www.cnto.org

China News

A news site updated daily with current issues in China. Includes the facility to search for previous articles and issues from past years
www.chinanews.cn

China.org.cn

A site containing news articles and links to promote China's businesses and developments
www.china.org.cn

China Today

A site containing a wealth of information about China. The site is regularly updated and can be used to access maps, articles and statistics about issues throughout China
www.chinatoday.com

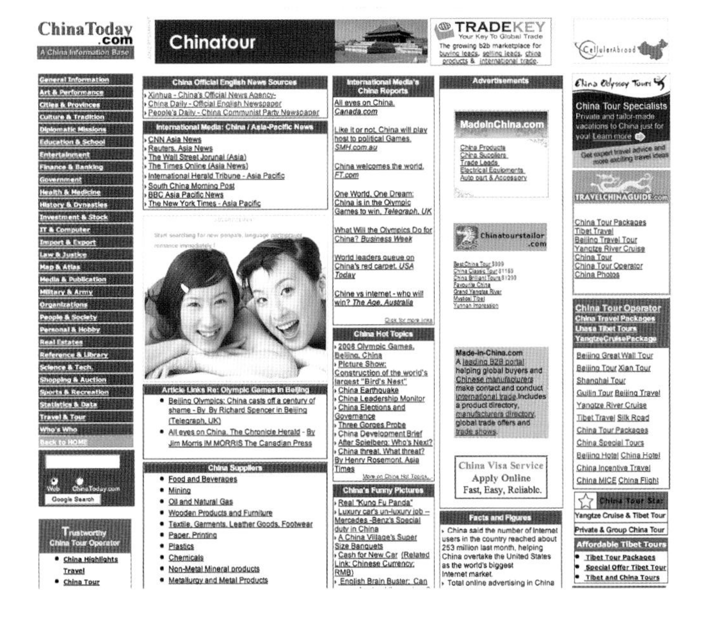

CPDRC

China's population information and research centre. Select 'English' section for detailed data and analysis of China's population changes, in many different sectors
www.cpirc.org.cn

Embassy of the People's Republic of China in the USA

China's embassy website, containing many links and articles about recent political changes in particular
www.china-embassy.org/eng

Hidden China

A tourist board site for China with a wealth of images, maps and up-to-date events in the more populated areas of China
www.hiddenchina.net

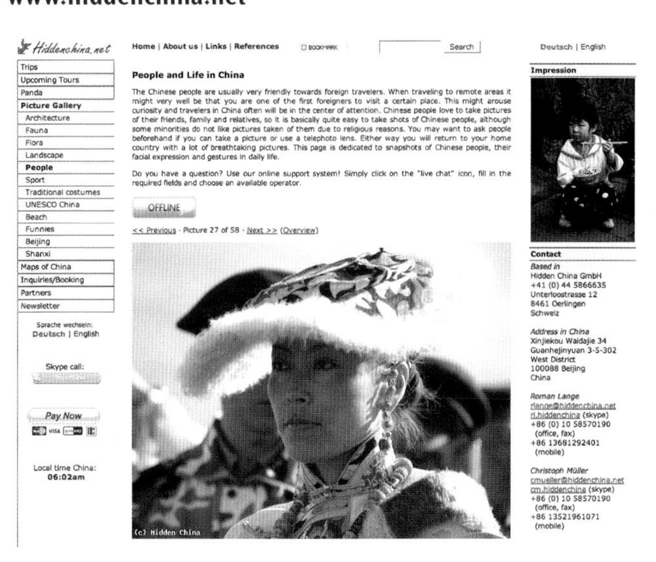

LESSON 3:

Where do people live in China?

Key questions

- Where do people live in China?
- Why do people choose to live in certain places?

Key words

- population
- population density
- densely populated
- sparsely populated
- population distribution

Resources

- Activity Sheet 6 (enlarged to A3 size)
- Information Sheet 2
- Activity Sheet 7
- Information Sheet 3
- Information Sheet 4
- Information Sheet 5
- Lego bricks (sugar cubes, marshmallows or coins may make suitable alternatives)
- Colouring pencils
- Atlases
- Digital camera

Learning objectives

- To be able to show on a map how population is distributed in China
- To understand why population in China is distributed this way

Assessment opportunities

- Students make a 3D population distribution map, then analyse it

Starter

Demonstrate, physically, the concept of population density in the classroom. Ask students to sit on desks – six on one desk, four on one desk, two on one desk, a few individuals on a desk each and some desks without students on. Use the demonstration to define the terms: population density, densely populated, sparsely populated and population distribution.

Main teaching and learning phase

Divide the class into groups of four. Tell students they are going to create a 3-dimensional population density map of China using Lego bricks.

Hand out copies of Activity Sheet 6 (enlarged to A3 size) and Information Sheet 2 to each group. They use Activity Sheet 6 as the base for the 3D map and read the instructions on Information Sheet 2. Give Lego bricks to each group – red bricks to represent each 20 people per square kilometre and white bricks to represent less than 20 people per square kilometre. You could demonstrate to students how to turn the population density data for one region into 3D on the map.

When each group has completed their map they should take a photograph of it (from an oblique vertical angle) for later use.

Students could then use these maps to create a 2D map of China's population by converting the number of bricks into a colour on a choropleth map.

> You could increase the complexity of the task for higher-attaining students, by giving them Information Sheet 3, which lists population density for all China's regions.

Hand out Information Sheet 4, or an atlas with a detailed map of China (you could also hand out Information Sheet 5 to help students get their tongues round some of the places they are investigating). Ask students to compare the map they have created with the detailed map. Discuss with the class why China's population is distributed this way, using the following questions:

- Which area is the most densely populated and why?
- Which area is the least densely populated and why?
- Why are some parts of China more densely populated than others?

Students write a paragraph to describe and explain China's population distribution. They should refer to the annotated maps from lesson 1, their 3D maps or their choropleth maps, to do this. They use the questions above as a structure for the paragraph.

Plenary/review

Give students the lists of cities and populations on Activity Sheet 7. You could do this on the whiteboard. Students match each city with the correct population. Then you can reveal the answers:

- London 12m
- Shanghai 17.5m
- Beijing 12.8m
- Mexico City 22.4m
- Canton 14.7m
- Newcastle 1m
- Birmingham 2.5m

Students use the answers to compare cities, helping them to develop a sense of scale. For example 'Shanghai is bigger than 17 Newcastles put together', or 'Beijing is bigger than London'.

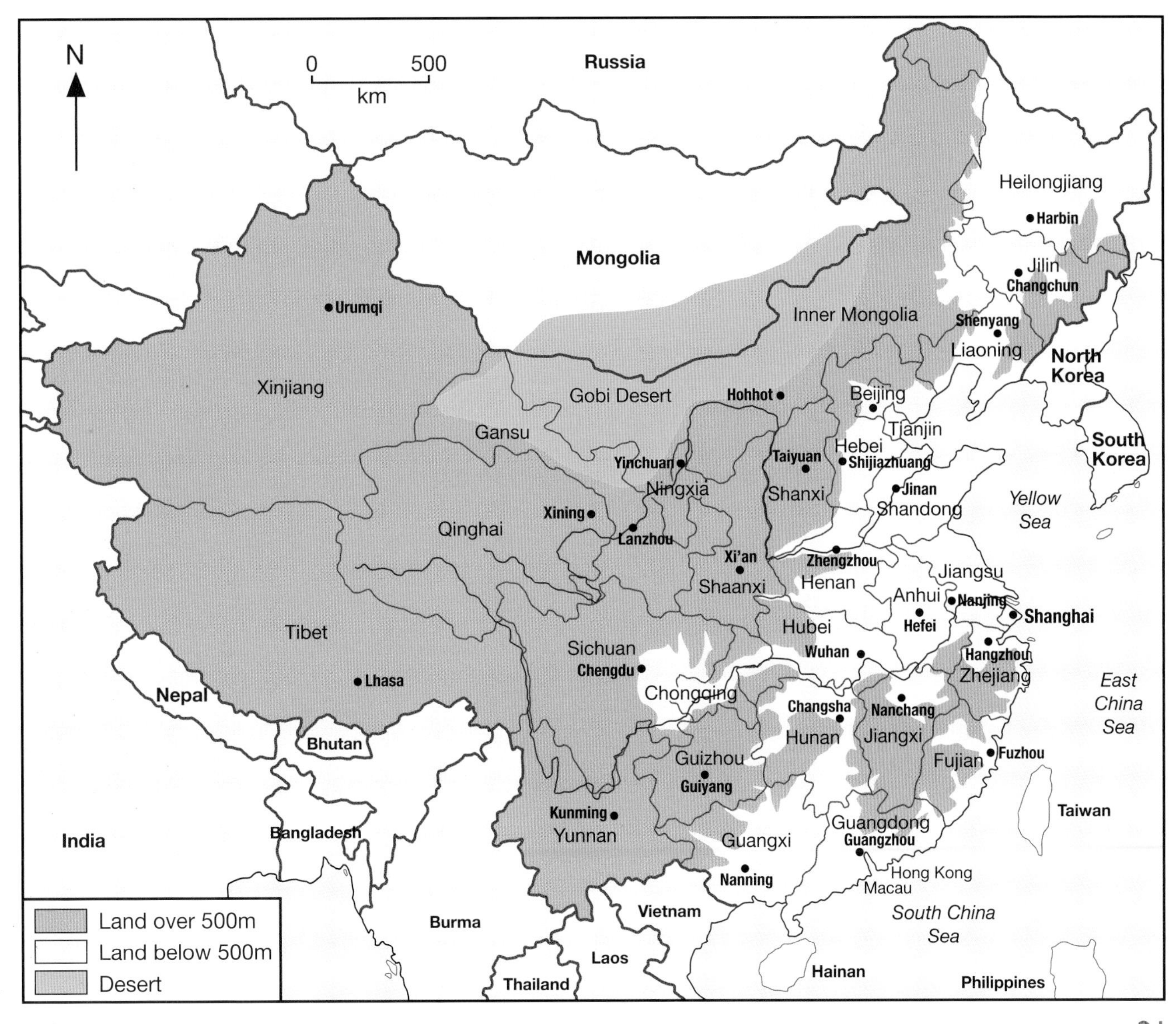

LESSON 4:

How is China linked with the rest of the world?

Key questions

- How is China linked with the rest of the world?

Key words

- more economically developed country (MEDC)
- less economically developed country (LEDC)

Resources

- Information Sheet 6
- Information Sheet 7
- Information Sheet 8
- Activity Sheet 8
- Atlases

Learning objectives

- To know how China is linked with other countries in the world
- To understand that closer relationships with other countries will aid China's development

Assessment opportunities

- Students explain how they are linked to China

Starter

Show students the photo of the Great Wall of China on Information Sheet 6. It would be good to have this on the whiteboard as they come into the class. Ask them to guess what it is, when it was built, how long it is and why it was built. The answers are on page 2 of the sheet. Use the photo to make the point that for most of China's history it was cut off from the rest of the world.

Then, read the first extract from Information Sheet 7 'China Shakes the World' aloud to the class. At the end, ask students to hypothesise why the pipeline is going to China. Then, read the second extract aloud to the class. This explains why the pipeline went to China. Ask students what contrast they notice between the Great Wall and this story.

Main teaching and learning phase

Give each student a copy of Information Sheet 8 and an A3 copy of Activity Sheet 8. Ask students to read about China's links with the rest of the world on the sheet. Then, on the blank world map, they draw a line between China and each country that it is linked with. They write a brief explanation of each link on the lines they have drawn. For example, for the link 'More of China's goods are exported to the USA than to any other country', students could write 'exports to USA' on that line.

> Higher-attaining students could classify and colour-code their lines. Classification is an important skill that helps students to organise ideas. In this case, it will help them to make more sense of China's many links with other countries.

When the map is completed, students join a partner to consider the following questions:

- Which countries have the most links with China?
- Why do these countries have so many links with China?
- How might the pattern of links shown on the map change in the future?

Plenary/review

Each student tells the rest of the class one way in which they are linked to China, by finishing the sentence: 'I am linked to China because…'. For example, they could say:

- I have travelled there
- I like Chinese food
- I have a member of family who lives there
- My clothes were made there.

> Tell students that they should try not to repeat the same idea that someone else has given. They could be increasingly creative in their responses. For example, they could say: 'The wire in our house is made from copper, mined in Zambia by a company from China'.

- More of China's goods are exported to the USA than to any other country
- China is in direct competition with countries such as Mexico for the manufacture of goods
- 2.4 million people from Russia visited China as tourists in 2006
- China borders Afghanistan, Bhutan, Burma, India, Kazakhstan, North Korea, Kyrgyzstan, Laos, Mongolia, Nepal, Pakistan, Russia, Tajikistan, Vietnam
- Many Chinese people migrated to the USA during the Gold Rush of the 1800s
- Brazil, Russia, India and China make up the BRIC countries, which are LEDCs that are quickly industrialising and improving their standards of living

Photo © Bryan Ledgard.

- 5% of Chinese tourists visited Europe in 2005 and this number is growing each year
- In 2004 the Chinese president announced that he was keen to develop stronger links with Africa. Africa earns a lot of money by buying minerals and energy resources from Africa.
- China and the USA are the world's biggest producers of CO_2
- Many students from China move to MEDCs such as the UK for their university education
- In 2007, China overtook Germany as the biggest car manufacturer in the world
- China imports more goods from Japan than any other country
- Africa supplies a third of China's crude oil imports, mainly from countries such as Chad, Nigeria and Sudan
- Many food items are prepared in China, including prawns from the UK which are sent to China to be shelled, before being flown back to supermarkets in the UK
- China exports a lot of its coal to South Korea and Japan
- Many businesses in Australia are investing in Chinese companies
- There are ongoing disputes about the border between China and India, which resulted in a war in 1962.
- China is investing heavily in copper mines in Zambia
- Chinese food is extremely popular in the USA and UK

LESSON 5:

How does China compare with other countries?

Key questions

- How does China compare with other countries?
- What are the characteristics of MEDCs and LEDCs?

Key words

- development
- Gross Domestic Product (GDP)

Resources

- Activity Sheet 9
- Activity Sheet 10
- Activity Sheet 11
- Information Sheet 9
- Information Sheet 10

Learning objectives

- To know the characteristics of MEDCs and LEDCs
- To be able to compare China's level of development with that of other countries

Assessment opportunities

- Students contribute to class discussion
- Students write a paragraph about development and how China compares with other countries

Starter

Students each work with a partner. Give each pair a copy of Activity Sheet 9 (or Activity Sheet 10 for higher-attaining students). For each indicator on the sheet, students decide whether a high or low score would represent a more developed country. An example has been completed for students.

For some categories (e.g. energy consumption) it may be difficult to decide whether a high or low score is 'more developed'. Tell students it is acceptable to have different opinions – the discussion surrounding the indicator is more important than the outcome itself.

Main teaching and learning phase

Students continue working in pairs. They use Activity Sheet 11 to play 'Top Trumps'. Students share the cards out between them and hold their cards in a pile in their hands. The aim of the game is to try to win all of the cards. One person chooses a category (e.g. life expectancy) for the top card in the pile and reads the 'score' aloud. The other person then reads the score for the card on the top of his or her own pile. The person with the best score for that category wins both cards, and puts them to the back of their pile. (The best score depends on what they decided for that category on Activity Sheet 9, not just the highest figure. For example, a foreign debt of 15 is better than a foreign debt of 44.) Students aim to win cards by choosing the category for which they think that the country is likely to be the most successful.

Higher attaining students may wish to make their own Top Trumps cards to use in the lesson. The table of indicators on Information Sheet 9 is provided to aid this activity.

After the activity, ask students to consider the question: 'How does China compare to the rest of the world?'. Students should think about this question for one minute, then discuss their ideas with a partner for two minutes. Finally, they share their ideas with the rest of the class. Encourage students to listen to each other's ideas, and to incorporate these into their own.

Students answer the following questions about development and how China compares with other countries. The questions become increasingly difficult. Students should aim to complete as many questions as possible in the time given:

- Which country was the most developed?
- Why was this country the most developed?
- What are the three main characteristics of MEDCs?
- What MEDC characteristics does China have?
- Does China have more of the characteristics of a MEDC or of a LEDC?

Plenary/review

Show students the Worldmapper map of wealth for 1990 on Information Sheet 10. You can do this on the interactive whiteboard. Explain that this map has been constructed to show the size of countries proportionate to their wealth. Ask students to identify the richest parts of the world, and the poorest. Into which category would they put China?

Now, show the map of wealth projected for 2015 so students can compare the two maps. Ask them to identify the main changes. They should notice that China's area grows dramatically, showing that its share of the world's wealth grows. Ask the students what impact this is likely to have on other aspects of China's development.

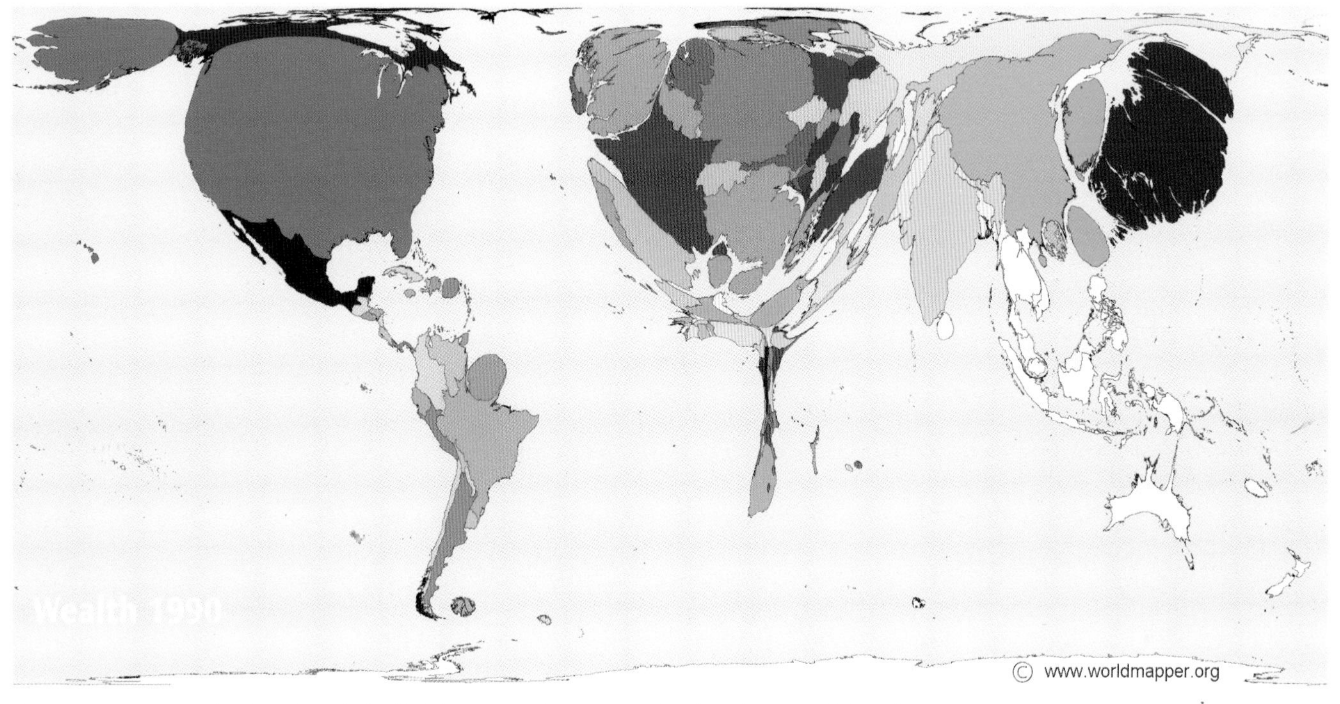

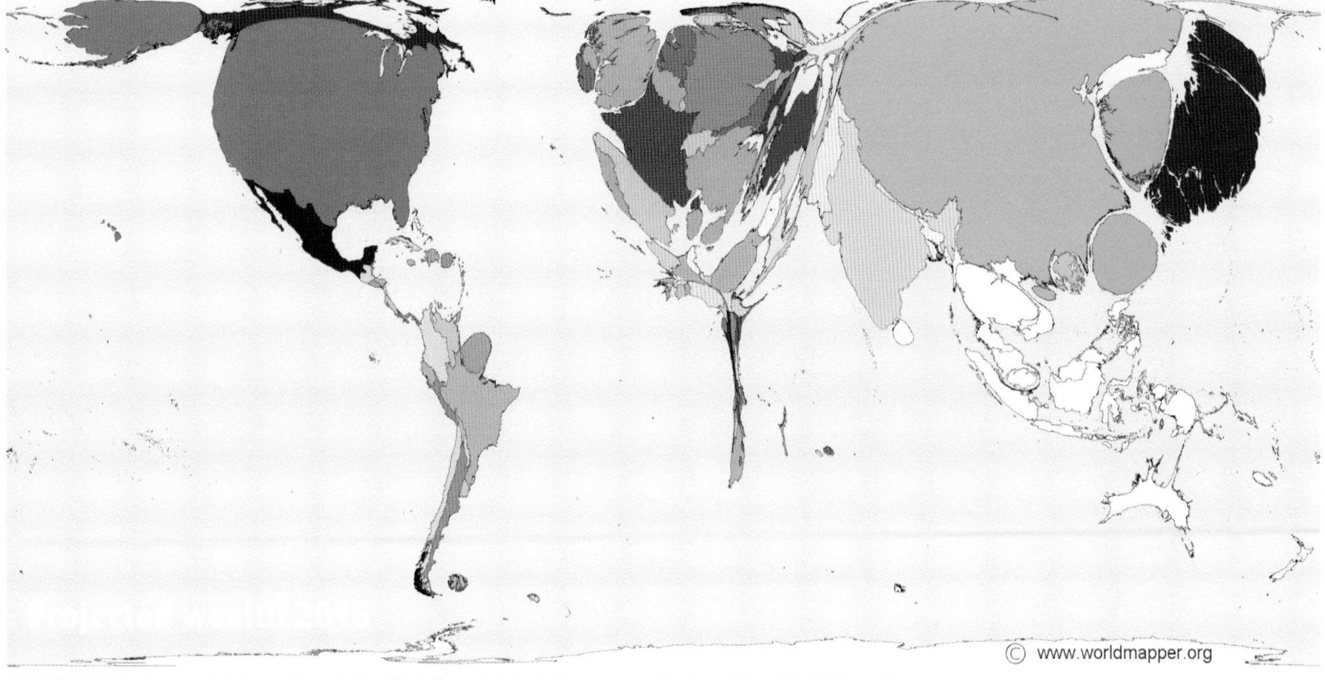

LESSON 6:
How is China developing?

Key question
- How is China developing?

Key words
- BRIC
- economic growth

Resources
- Figure 3 from CD
- Activity Sheet 12
- Activity Sheet 13
- Information Sheet 11
- Figures 4-10 from CD

Learning objectives
- To be able to recognise evidence of China's development
- To understand how China's economy is likely to change in the future

Assessment opportunities
- Students present a photostory to illustrate how China is developing

Starter
Show Figure 3 to the class on the whiteboard. Discuss the meaning of the cartoon with the class. Ask students to think about what the money that China is earning could be used for, and which aspects of the country (e.g. education, landscape, healthcare etc.) this may help to improve.

Figure 3: China's race with the world.

Main teaching and learning phase
Show students Figures 4-10 on an interactive whiteboard (the same images are on Activity Sheet 12). Ask students what evidence of development in China they can see in the photos.

Cartoons are a good way to get students thinking. Often the meaning is hidden below the surface. Encourage students to look for deeper meaning within this cartoon and ask them to note three key ideas.

Now, give students a copy of Activity Sheet 12. They work in pairs to match statements and photographs. Students cut out the statements and photographs and then arrange them into a photostory to answer the question: What evidence is there that China is becoming more developed? Higher-attaining students can also answer the question: Is economic growth the same as development?

Students use the statements to illustrate their photostory, but can also add their own ideas and opinions. At the end of this activity each pair presents their photostory to the rest of the class.

This activity would benefit from the use of ICT. Students could use PowerPoint to make their presentations. They could also add their own images sourced from the internet.

Plenary/review
Show students the graph on Activity Sheet 13. Again, you could do this on the interactive whiteboard. The graph shows when the BRIC economies are likely to overtake those of MEDCs. Explain that currently the USA is the world's biggest economy, Japan second and Germany third (you will find some useful supporting information on Information Sheet 11). Discuss the questions on the sheet to ensure that students are able to interpret the graph. Do they think the predictions on the graph are likely to happen? And, from what they know about China, why do they think this is?

Häagen-Dazs
玲珑轩

同一个世界 同一个梦想
Beijing 2008
One World One Dream

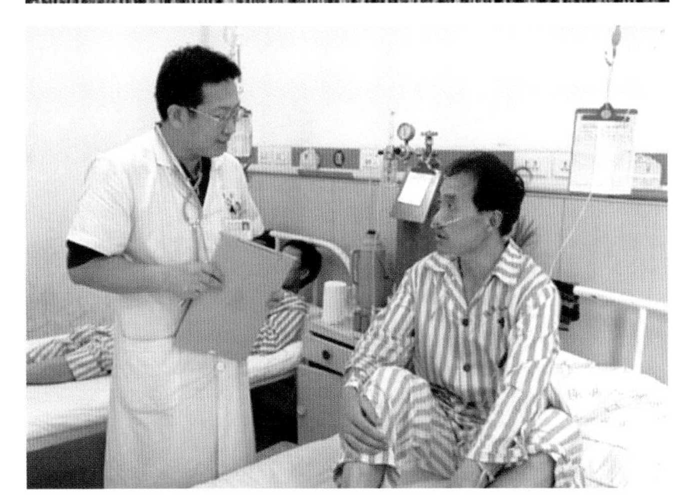

Figures 4-10

LESSON 7:

How sustainable is China's development?

Key questions

- How sustainable is China's development?
- What is sustainability?

Key words

- sustainable
- sustainability

Resources

- Activity Sheet 14
- Information Sheet 12
- Activity Sheet 15
- Red and green pens/pencils
- Activity Sheet 16
- Activity Sheet 17

Learning objectives

- To understand the concept of sustainability
- To know the advantages and disadvantages of the Three Gorges Dam project
- To be able to form a balanced opinion about an issue

Assessment opportunities

- Students write their balanced opinion of the Three Gorges Dam project

Starter

Divide the class into small groups. Hand out Activity Sheet 14 to students. Students read the different definitions of sustainability on the sheet and discuss these in groups for two minutes. Each group then writes their own definition of sustainability. The groups share their definitions with the whole class. You could ask the class to vote for the definition they like the most.

Main teaching and learning phase

Show students the photos of the Three Gorges Dam Project on Information Sheet 12. You could show these on the whiteboard. What questions would students like to ask about the project? Make a list of the questions for them to refer to as they read the article on Activity Sheet 15.

Hand out Activity Sheets 15 and 16. As they read the article about the Three Gorges Dam project on Activity Sheet 15, students underline the advantages of the project in green, and the disadvantages in red. They may also find the answers to some of the questions they asked.

When students have underlined the article, they list the advantages and disadvantages on Activity Sheet 16. They compare the balance of advantages and disadvantages on the scales, then give their own balanced opinion. Encourage students to refer to sustainability in their answers, using the definition they constructed at the start of the lesson. Lower attaining students can use Activity Sheet 17 to help them to structure their opinions.

Students often find it difficult to write a balanced opinion. They tend to take one side or the other, and not see alternative points of view. Weighing up the arguments for and against the Three Gorges Dam will help them to do this.

Plenary/review

Invite students to read their opinions aloud to the class.

As students listen to each other, ask them to respect the fact that each person may have different opinions. After listening, they might even want to change their own opinion!

The Three Gorges Dam Project

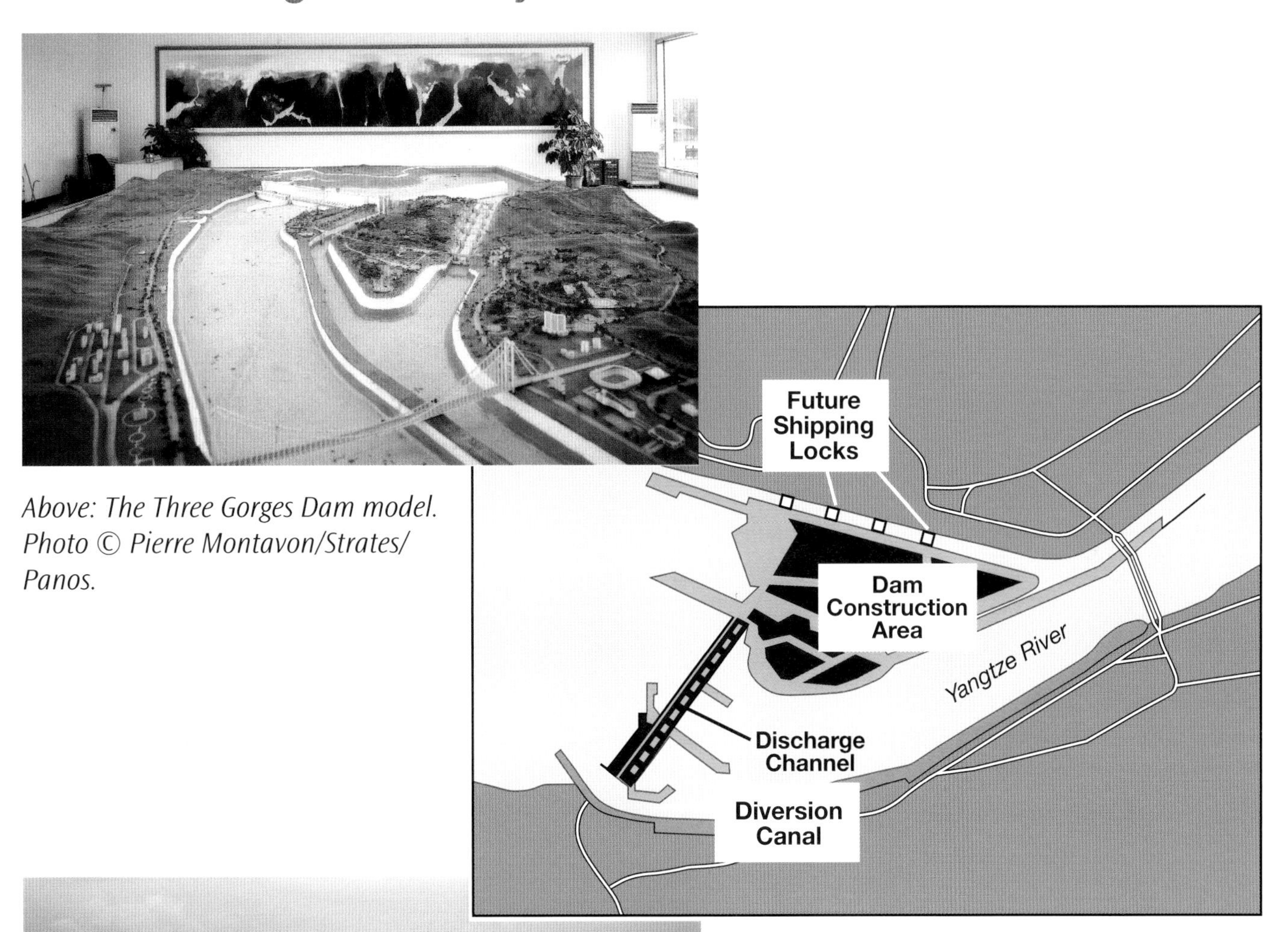

Above: The Three Gorges Dam model. Photo © Pierre Montavon/Strates/Panos.

Above: A plan of the Dam.

Above: Tourism at the Three Gorges Dam. Photo © Espen Rasmussen/Panos.

Right: Before the Dam – the white sign on the left of the image shows where the water would rise to. Photo: Margaret Mackintosh.

LESSON 8:

Is there a more sustainable option for China?

Key questions
- Is there a more sustainable option for China?

Key words
- sustainable development

Resources
- Information Sheet 13
- Activity Sheet 18
- London cartoon at http://hello.eboy.com/eboy/?p=197

Learning objectives
- To understand how the Dongtan Eco-City project is designed to be sustainable
- To be able to critically evaluate the Dongtan Eco-City project

Assessment opportunities
- Students write a letter to describe the city of Dongtan and evaluate the project

Starter
Tell students that they are going to work in pairs to try to solve a Chinese mystery: How will rice husks make China more sustainable? Hand out sets of cards from Activity Sheet 18 to each pair.

Students begin by sorting the cards into categories, according to the information they provide (e.g. China in general, buildings, Dongtan). They may choose the categories themselves, but all cards must be put into a category. Students feed back their ideas to the class. Discuss possible solutions to the mystery question with the class.

Main teaching and learning phase
Show the students Dongtan's location and the artist's impressions on Information Sheet 13. You could show this on the whiteboard. Students are now going to write a letter from a teenager in China who is moving to Dongtan. They imagine they are writing the letter to a friend, describing what they think the city will be like. The letter should include:
- What the main aims of the Dongtan Eco-City are
- What the city will look like
- What measures the city has taken to become environmentally sustainable
- What will be good about living in Dongtan
- What will be difficult about living in Dongtan
- Whether Dongtan is sustainable or not, in the student's opinion.

They use the information on the mystery cards, the location map and the artist's impressions on Information Sheet 13 to help them write the letter.

> When students undertake an extended writing task, it is important that they know the purpose of their writing and the audience they are writing for. You could model the style of writing for them.

Plenary/review
Show the class the cartoon image of London from the eboy website on the interactive whiteboard. Ask students to find as many ways as possible to change London to make it more sustainable (e.g. put solar panels on the roof, fewer cars etc.). Make a list of all the ideas. Encourage students to think of the ways in which London is a less sustainable city than Dongtan. Is it possible to make existing cities, like London, more sustainable? Or is the only way to start afresh, like Dongtan?

> A suitable homework follow-up for this lesson would be to ask students to research a small-scale project, perhaps closer to home, and assess it's sustainability. A good example would be the BedZED project in south-west London (www.peabody.org.uk). Or you could give the class a choice of examples to research. This will put the scale and impact of the Dongtan Eco-City project into perspective.

Images courtesy of Arup

LESSON 9:

Should China try to reduce its energy consumption?

Key questions
- Should China try to reduce its energy consumption?
- How are economy, population and energy consumption linked?

Key words
- energy consumption
- greenhouse gas emissions

Resources
- Information Sheet 14
- Space (in classroom or outside) to make an opinion line
- Information Sheet 15
- Information Sheet 16

Learning objectives
- To know the world's biggest economies, populations and consumers of energy
- To understand how the economy, population and energy consumption are linked
- To be able to express opinions about levels of energy consumption

Assessment opportunities
- Students write a speech on how the UK should respond to China's energy consumption levels

Starter
Ask students try to guess the top ten countries for wealth, population and energy consumption. Information Sheet 14 has the answers. You could split the class into two teams. Teams take it in turns to guess the countries. Each team gets one point for every correct answer. Every incorrect answer results in the other team being allowed to have an extra guess. First, ask students to try to guess the top ten richest countries. When they have guessed these, they go on to guess the countries with the highest population and energy consumption.

As students guess the correct answers, record the information on the board. By the end of the activity you should have three completed lists (from Information Sheet 14). Ask students to compare the lists. What similarities or differences can they see? How can they explain these?

It may take a while for students to process the information in front of them. Allow them 'thinking' time – this could be achieved by playing a piece of music while students think, to focus their minds and prevent distractions.

Now, show students similar information visually on Information Sheet 15. It shows world maps of energy consumption and population. You could show this on the interactive whiteboard. Discuss the questions below:
- Which countries consume more than their share of the world's energy?
- Which countries consume less than their share?
- How do the UK's and China's energy consumption compare with their population?
- Do they think that any countries have the 'right' to consume greater amounts of energy than others?

Main teaching and learning phase
Discuss opinions briefly. Start with some easy examples, e.g. 'I like chocolate' (expect most students to strongly agree!); 'I think that we should have more homework' (expect most students to strongly disagree!).

Read the list of opinions on Information Sheet 14 to the class, one at a time, and ask students to decide to what extent they agree with each statement. Choose a suitable open place (e.g. the front of a classroom, the playground) where students will be able to stand in a line. Tell them to move to the point on the line that best represents their opinion. One end of the line represents people who strongly agree with a statement, and the other represents people who strongly disagree. If students are neutral or balanced in their opinion they stand in the middle. They discuss their opinions with the people next to them in the line to see if they are in the correct position.

To avoid confrontation within the group, remind students that everyone is entitled to a different opinion, and reinforce the principle that it is acceptable to change your opinion if you wish to do so. Students often feel pressured to have an opinion when they have not yet formed one, so it is important to have trust and flexibility within the teaching group.

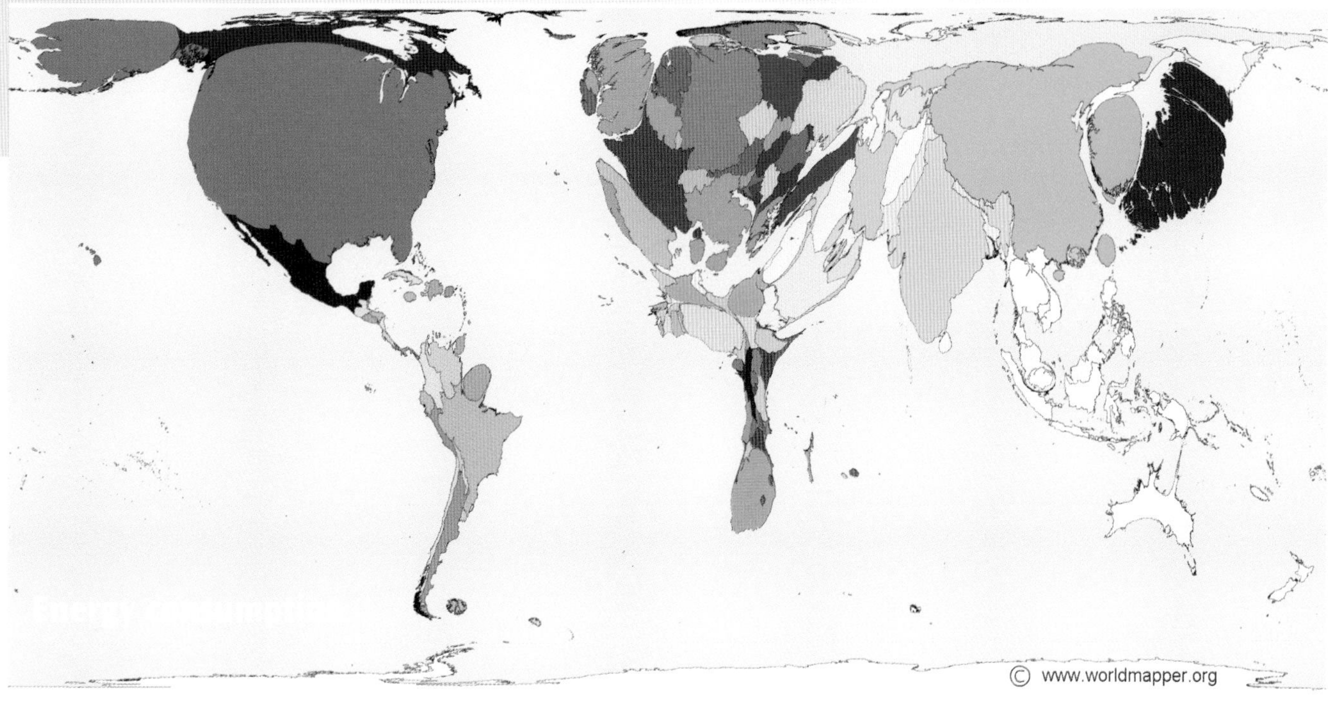

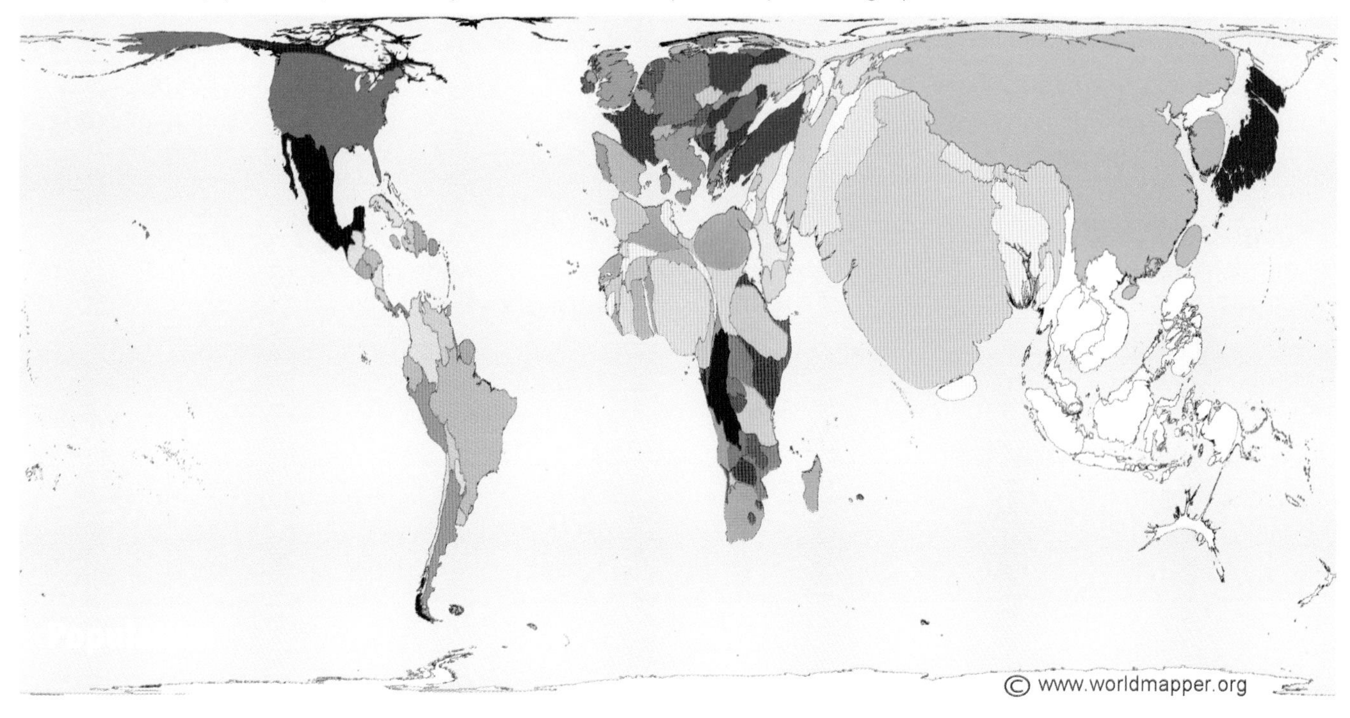

After all the students are in a line, ask individuals to explain their choice of position. Offer students the opportunity to change their position in the line after discussion.

Ask students to write a short speech for the UK's Prime Minister to give, explaining how the government is going to respond to China's greenhouse gas emissions. The speech should be 100-200 words in length, and should explain:

- Why China produces so many greenhouse gases
- What the UK intends to do about this (even if nothing)
- Why the UK has decided to take this action.

> Students may choose to 'do nothing' about China's greenhouse gas emissions – this is a valid answer, but they must explain their reasons in full.

Plenary/review

Invite a few students to read their speeches to the class. Try to choose students with different opinions. Then tell students about the Kyoto Protocol. You can find out more about this on Information Sheet 16. Ask students to compare their opinions with the Kyoto Protocol. Was the Kyoto Protocol a good idea? Did it go far enough? How could it be developed in future?

LESSON 10:

How and why is China likely to change in the future?

Key questions

- How and why is China likely to change in the future?
- What will geography teachers say about China in 20 years' time?

Key words

- sustainability
- environmental
- political
- interdependence

Resources

- Copy of list of country characteristics created during the starter activity in lesson 1
- A3 paper for mind map
- Information Sheet 17
- Information Sheet 18

Learning objectives

- To understand how China's characteristics might change
- To understand how China's relationship with other countries may change in the future

Assessment opportunities

- Students contribute to class discussion on how China may change
- Students create a mind map to show how China's characteristics might change

Main teaching and learning phase

Show students the pairs of images of China on Information Sheet 17. Ask students what the link is between each pair of photographs, and how it shows that China is changing. See Information Sheet 18 for a brief description for each pair of photographs.

Although Information Sheet 18 explains how the photographs are linked, students may suggest other ideas that are equally valid. Incorporate as many different 'links' into the discussion as possible.

Now, refer students back to the work they did in lesson 1. During that lesson they made a class list of 'characteristics that make a place' and put them into categories. Ask students to create a mind map for China using these categories. They write information about each category to say how and why China is changing, and may change in the future.

Plenary/review

Ask students to imagine that they are teaching a geography lesson about China 20 years in the future. Invite some students to the front of the class with their mind maps. They use the mind map to describe the changes in China. Ask the rest of the class to decide whose description they think is most likely to happen and to give reasons for their opinion. You could ask the class to vote on the most likely future for China.

Great Wall of China + McDonald's – this pair shows the difference between a China that initially built a wall to exclude the rest of the world, and protect itself from it, but which is now embracing the rest of the world through capitalism in order to develop.

Photo © Margaret Mackintosh.

Photo © Mark Storey.

Traditional Farming + Air Pollution in China – This pair demonstrates the changes in employment from the primary to secondary sector. It also highlights the environmental degradation as a result of China's industrialisation.

Photo © Margaret Mackintosh.

Photo © Mark Storey.

Traditional Chinese food + Starbuck's etc in square – This pair shows the changes in culture (from inward, to outward looking) that have occurred as a result of China's increasing interdependence with other parts of the world (particularly the West).

Photo © Adam Nichols.

Photo © Mark Storey.

Traffic in Xiamen + Bicycle Park – these two modern images show the two sides of China's environmental attitude – on one hand, the traffic in cities is polluting, but on the other hand, China is very forward-thinking and is moving towards sustainable options, like bicycles.

Photo © Adam Nichols.

Photo © Bryan Ledgard.

Traditional board game + Lady collecting water bottles – this pair illustrates the contrasts in modern Chinese culture. Some aspects of Chinese culture are well-preserved, while other aspects (e.g. environmental attitudes) are changing. This pair demonstrates that it is possible for China to adapt, without completely changing its culture and history.

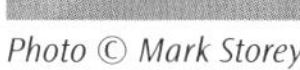
Photo © Mark Storey.

Photo © Mark Storey.

4: GLOSSARY

BRIC – Brazil, Russia, India and China: a group of four countries who are developing much more rapidly than other LEDCs through high levels of investment

densely populated – an area where a relatively large number of people live in a given space

development – growth or advancement

economy – a system of producing, distributing and consuming wealth (In this unit, the term 'economy' largely applies to that of countries)

economic growth – the increase of wealth in a country as it earns money by producing more goods and services

energy consumption – the amount of energy used

environment – the physical landscape of a place

environmental – relating to the environment

GDP – Gross Domestic Product: The sum total of goods and services produced by an area (usually a country) in a given year. Usually expressed in US Dollars

greenhouse gas emissions – gas released into the atmosphere which contributes to global warming

human – relating to human-made things

interdependence – the relationships between countries which determine that they are reliant upon each other for trade and wealth

LEDC – Less Economically Developed Country

MEDC – More Economically Developed Country

migration – The movement of people from one place to another

NIC – Newly Industrialising Country

physical – relating to the natural world

political – relating to government or state affairs

population – The amount of people living in an area (usually a country) at a given time

population density – the number of people living in an area per square kilometre (on average)

population distribution – the location of the population across the country or area

relevance – if something has a bearing on the issue

reliability – how much something can be depended upon

source – where something originates from

sparsely populated – an area where relatively few people live in a given amount of space

sustainability – see various definitions in starter for Lesson 7

sustainable – something that continues without being wasteful or damaging

sustainable development – development that meets present and future needs

5: LINKS FOR FURTHER IDEAS AND RESOURCES

Websites

China
An on-line encyclopaedic account of China and its history. The site contains many useful links to articles and websites for further research. Please be aware that wikipedia entries are contributed by the public, and are not closely regulated *http://en.wikipedia.org/wiki/China*

China National Tourist Office
China's official tourist site. Contains information about new developments in China's tourist industry, as well as introductory information on the country *www.cnto.org*

China News
A news site updated daily with current issues in China. Includes the facility to search for previous articles and issues from past years *www.chinanews.cn*

China.org.cn
A site containing news articles and links to promote China's businesses and developments *www.china.org.cn*

China Today
A site containing a wealth of information about China. The site is regularly updated and can be used to access maps, articles and statistics about issues throughout China *www.chinatoday.com*

CPDRC
China's population information and research centre. Select 'English' section for detailed data and analysis of China's population changes, in many different sectors *www.cpirc.org.cn*

Embassy of the People's Republic of China in the USA
China's embassy website, containing many links and articles about recent political changes in particular *www.china-embassy.org/eng*

Hidden China
A tourist board site for China with a wealth of images, maps and up-to-date events in the more populated areas of China *www.hiddenchina.net*

References and further reading

Balderstone, D. (ed) (2006) *Secondary Geography Handbook*. Sheffield: Geographical Association.

Barford, D. and Dorling, D. (2006). 'Worldmapper: The world as you've never seen it before', *Teaching Geography*, 31, 2, pp. 68-75.

Chow, C-S. (2005) 'Cultural Diversity and Tourism Development in Yunnan Province, China', *Geography*, 90, 3, pp. 294-303.

Davison, G. (2006) 'Start at the beginning', *Teaching Geography*, 31, 3, pp. 105-8.

Durbin, C. (2006) 'Media literacy and geographical imaginations' in Balderstone, D. (ed) *Secondary Geography Handbook*. Sheffield: Geographical Association, pp. 226-37.

The Economist (2007) *Pocket World in Figures 2007*. London: Profile Books.

Frean, P. (2005) 'What's this got to do with me?', *Teaching Geography*, 30, 1, pp. 32-3.

Geographical Association (2005) *Teaching Geography: Valuing Places*. 30, 1. Sheffield: Geographical Association.

Goldman Sachs (2003) *Dreaming with BRICs: The path to 2050*. www2.goldmansachs.com/ideas/brics/book/99-dreaming.pdf (viewed 18/07/08).

Jackson, J. (2005) 'Sharing Places', *Teaching Geography*, 30, 1, pp. 28-31

Kynge, J. (2006) *China Shakes the World*. London: Phoenix.

Lambert, D., Gardner, D. and Swift, D. (2007) 'Key Stage 3 Review Special: The changes ahead', *Teaching Geography*, 32, 1, pp. 5-12.

Morgan, J. (2006) 'Geography: A dynamic subject' in Balderstone, D. (ed) *Secondary Geography Handbook*. Sheffield: Geographical Association, pp. 38-45.

Wang, D. (2005) 'Issues in Yunnan Province: An introduction', *Geography*, 90, 3, p. 278.

Wellsted, E. (2006) 'Understanding distant places' in Balderstone, D. (ed) *Secondary Geography Handbook*. Sheffield: Geographical Association, pp. 60-9.

6: ASSESSMENT FRAMEWORK: Where does China go from here?

Level 7-8

- Students are aware of the different identities of places within China, and can give reasons for this variety
- Students can describe the positive and negative impacts of China's development on its population, wealth and relationships with other countries

Level 5-6

- Students have a good understanding of China's geographical location and context, and can relate this to other aspects of China

Level 3-4

- Students are aware of the location and context of China
- Students can describe human and physical features of China
- Students understand simple examples of sustainable and unsustainable development in China
- Students can suggest simple ideas about how China will change in the future

- Students can explain how population, wealth and international relationships will affect China's development in the future
- Students can evaluate large issues such as sustainable development and offer their own opinion of individual examples
- Students are aware that China is changing, and can give reasons for this change
- Students can appreciate bias and relevance of information, by assessing its source
- Students describe the sustainable and unsustainable elements of China's development in some detail, and offer solutions to how development could become more sustainable in the future
- Students can make detailed predictions of how China may change in the future, and explain how these changes will affect both China and other countries that it is linked to

PoS coverage in the *Toolkit* series

		Into Africa	Rise and Rise of China	British or European ?	Look at it this way	Water works	Thorny issue	Faster, higher, stronger	Changing my world	Moving stories	Future floods
KEY CONCEPTS	Place	✓	✓	✓	★	★	★	✓	★	★	✓
	Space	★	★	★	✓	✓	★	✓	★	✓	
	Scale	★	★	★	★	★	★	★	✓	★	★
	Interdependence	✓	✓	★		★	✓		★	★	
	Physical human process		★		✓	★	✓	✓	✓	✓	★
	Environmental interaction	★	✓		✓	✓		★	✓		✓
	Diversity	✓		✓	★		★	★		✓	
KEY PROCESSES	Enquiry	✓	✓	✓	✓	✓	✓	✓	✓	✓	✓
	Fieldwork				★						✓
	Graphicacy	★	★	✓	★	★		★	★	✓	✓
	Communication	★		★	★	★	★	✓	★	★	
RANGE AND CONTENT	Variety of scale	★		★		★		★	✓	★	
	Location	★	★	✓	★		★	★			★
	Aspects of UK			✓	★			✓	★	✓	✓
	Parts of the world	✓	✓	✓		✓	✓		★		
	Physical geography				✓	★	★				★
	Human geography	✓	★	★				★		✓	
	People-environment	★	✓		✓	✓	★	★	✓		✓
CURRICULUM OPPORTUNITIES	Personal experience	★		✓	★	★	★		★	★	
	Contemporary context	✓	✓	★	★	★	★	✓	★	★	★
	Enquiry approaches	★	★	★	★	★	✓	★	★	★	
	Maps & GIS	★	★	★	★	★	★	★	★	★	✓
	Fieldwork				★						✓
	Responsible action	★		✓		★	✓	★	✓		
	Issues in the news	★	✓	★	★	✓		✓	✓	✓	✓
	Use of ICT				✓		★	★	★		★
	Curriculum links			★	★	★	★	★		✓	

KEY: ✓ major focus/fully developed ★ additional aspect